YOU ARE BRIL

—NIKKO

To my best friend... My loving wife, Vanessa.

Copyright © 2017 by Nikkolas Smith

All rights reserved. No part of this book may be reproduced in any manner without the express written consent of the publisher, except in the case of brief exerpts in critical reviews or articles.
All inquiries should be addressed to VJS Productions, P.O. Box 11729, Spring, TX 77391-1729
www.VJSproductions.com

Written & Illustrated By Nikkolas Smith
www.NIKKOLAS.com

Print ISBN: 978-0-9723658-0-2

Printed in the United States of America

My name is Jakkie...
but you may know me as Princess Poofy!
...of the Majestic Curly-Q Queendom.

I didn't rise to this royal position simply because I was born here...

Nope... I'm Princess because of my gifted ability to make decisions....

Even though I'm older now, and much wiser, I still have to make tough decisions every day...

"Honey with PB&J? That's okay..."

One day, I was reading up on a nearby Queendom known as the Strawberry-Plum Paradise.

Home to the Strawberry-Plum Princess...
And her magical Spider-Silk hair...
I mean just look at how
it waves wildly in
the breeze!

That's when
I decided to
try her
hairstyle
too!

I said "Mom, my hair is SUPER THICK! It won't fly free like Strawberry-Plum-Spider-Silk hair... ...can you press it?"

It came out nice though...
I've decided this silky hairstyle is okay!
It's nice to have options...

As you can see by her silky waterfall locks, she's a royal descendant of the Strawberry-Plum Paradise.

Kim and I are best friends...

And tonight is the last summer sleepover before school starts again!

When Kim and I arrived to the first day of school, we realized how many different characteristics (and HAIRSTYLES!) there are in the world. We all have unique features that help describe us!

Sometimes we use our features to describe each other, which is okay!
You may even have a nickname based on one of your traits...
Embrace your traits... it's what makes you unique!

MUST BE THIS TALL

...or short...

...or tall...

...or wearing glasses...

...or having thicker hair!
(that's okay!)

...or even any skin color.

The choices you make, and the actions you take, are the things that tell everyone who you are.

Nikkolas Smith, a native of Houston, Texas, is a Master of Architecture recipient from Hampton University, Children's Book Author/Illustrator, and Theme Park Designer. His first picture book, "The Golden Girls of Rio" was nominated for an NAACP Image Award. He also creates freelance concept art, activist art paintings, and Hollywood movie posters. After hours, Nikkolas leads in youth mentoring on Saturdays, with the kids of Compton & Watts, CA, giving lessons in digital painting and life skills for success.
www.NIKKOLAS.com